WHAT IS YOUR HEART
LONGING FOR?

He's the King of all kings,
yet his crown was not
what you would think.
He chose the crown of mocking,
the crown of scorn,
the crown of thorns.
And he did it all
for you...

The Little Books of Why™

WHY A CROWN?

Bodie & Brock Thoene

PARABLE
SAN LUIS OBISPO, CALIFORNIA
OUTREACH
VISTA, CALIFORNIA

The Little Books of Why™ by Bodie and Brock Thoene are produced by Parable, 3563 Empleo Street, San Luis Obispo, CA 93401 and Outreach, Inc., 2230 Oak Ridge Way, Vista, CA 92081. Visit parable.com or outreach.com.

Printed in the United States of America
12 11 10 09 08 07
7 6 5 4 3 2 1

CONTENTS

INTRODUCTION

EASTER MORNING
1965

*The story is forever
engraved on my heart.*

Bodie Thoene

It was a story I was never meant to know. My mother's sorrow—the story of a battle lost and a war that was won. The truth was a personal wound, profound and deep, yet Mama bore it with tremendous dignity throughout her long and wonderful life.

"Why don't I have a grandpa to come to school on grandparent's day?" I had asked her when I was in first grade. "How did your Pop die?"

"Pop died of...it was his heart," Mama had answered me.

Sooner or later, I suppose it was inevitable that the facts would come out. I was the first of all the kids in our family to know. I did not speak of it to anyone for fifteen years until the day Mama sat my siblings down and told them what had happened to her father.

I learned the truth on Easter morning, 1965. I was fourteen when I visited my grandfather's grave during my first trip to Akron, Ohio, with my mother and father.

The cemetery where Pop was buried was like a garden. Groups of people in bright Easter clothes, like bouquets of living flowers, encircled the last resting places of loved ones.

So many flowers. So many broken hearts. So many memories.

A life-sized stone cross in a shelter

portrayed the suffering of Jesus. Spikes pierced His clawlike hands and twisted feet. His agonized gaze turned heavenward as if the sculptor had captured the moment Jesus cried out, "My God, My God! Why have you forsaken me?"

The crown of thorns was shoved deep into the flesh of his torn brow. The plaque above His head read: "King of the Jews."

Mama paused and bowed her head to pray briefly at the foot of the cross. It was as if the picture of Christ's suffering somehow gave her strength and courage to lead my father and me to where Pop was buried.

Even after twenty years she found the place easily. "Here." Tears filled her eyes as she knelt and brushed away grass clippings from his name. "Hello, Pop."

All the wonderful stories Mama had told us about her Pop came to my mind. Pictures of the tall, handsome man in his white straw hat came to life for me. Suddenly I realized that Pop was more than just a name in

Mama's stories. Pop had been a real person. Her daddy. He had been someone she had loved very much.

"I haven't been back here in twenty years, but I think of him every day," Mama said quietly as she adjusted a small American flag in the ground and laid down a woven wreath of yellow roses. "Bodie, he would have loved you. He was the kindest man…the kindest…a poet…like you." Her voice trailed away. Then she linked arms with my father and said lovingly, as if to introduce him to her father, "Pop, if only…if only you could have met my husband, Tommy. And our little Bo. Your other grandchildren are home in California. Pop, I have such a wonderful life. I'm really happy. Like you wanted me to be."

The engraving on the black granite stone identified Pop as a veteran of World War I. Other than that, there was only his name, birth date, and the day, month, and year of his death, twenty years before, in 1945.

As we stood there quietly, I did the math

between Pop's birth and death. "Mama! He was only 46," I remarked, surprised that Pop had died so young. "You're almost the age he was when he…"

She nodded as my father put his arm around her shoulders. Mama replied, "I never thought of that. I've lived longer than my pop. He was young, wasn't he?"

"Wow," I said. "A heart attack so young?"

My father shifted uncomfortably at my words. I sensed, as I had many times before, that I did not know the whole story of my grandfather's death or why Mama left the memories of Akron behind to make a new life in Bakersfield, California.

Mama answered in a whisper. "No. Not a heart attack. It was a long, fierce battle. And in the end, Pop died…of a broken heart. The war—so much suffering and loss all around us. The world, his life, was so harsh. He lost hope."

Suddenly, the reality of her words came crashing in on my consciousness.

Pop, the kindest man…gentle, good…the heart of a poet…my mother's dear Pop…

After a long silence she clasped my hand. We walked slowly back to the shelter, where the crown of thorns on the head of the suffering Jesus seemed to be the emblem of all suffering.

"You understand what I mean, don't you?" Mama asked.

I swallowed hard and nodded. Only at the foot of the cross could I dare to ask, "What really happened?"

She shared only a few of the tragic details. The war. Pop's crippling illness. Her mother's courage. The end. There would be much more she would reveal over the years as I grew to adulthood, and we shared our hearts with one another. But that morning she kissed the top of my head, hugged me, and looked up into the face of Jesus.

Her voice did not tremble when she spoke, though her eyes brimmed with emotion.

"Twenty years ago, after Pop's funeral, I stood right here and I asked God about suffering. Every day life seemed to be an unending battle, a war no one could win. So many wonderful young men we loved died on distant battle-fields. Then Pop...here. I looked up at the crown of thorns and asked God why Jesus, such a kind Savior, had to wear a crown of thorns. *Why?* I asked. *Why is there such terrible suffering and sadness in the world? In our own lives?* Life seemed so unfair even for the Son of God. A crown of thorns? Why should it be? We were created to live in a joyful place. Created to live in a perfect garden. God never meant for there to be thorns in His creation."

Even at my young age, I knew she was somehow speaking of her own suffering and the suffering of my grandfather. I clasped her hand as if she were, at that moment, my sister.

Gaze fixed on Jesus, she lifted her chin. "It took me twenty years of searching after

Pop died to find the answers to my questions. It took twenty years for me to finally understand why Jesus wore that crown of thorns. It means something, you know. It really, really means something."

WHY A CROWN?

*What kind of crown
are you seeking?*

Crown Him with many crowns,
the Lamb upon His throne.
Hark! How the heavenly anthem drowns
all music but its own.
Awake, my soul, and sing
of Him who died for thee,
And hail Him as thy matchless King
through all eternity.

—"CROWN HIM WITH MANY CROWNS"
VERSE 1, WORDS BY MATTHEW BRIDGES, 1852

SEEKING #1 . . .

When you think of a *crown*, what images come to your mind? A magnificent headpiece, glittering with gold, rubies, and diamonds? Something that a king or queen would wear? Or perhaps an artifact in a museum?

Most of us associate the word *crown* with royalty. A king or queen wears a crown as the emblem of his or her authority, a visible expression of the right to reign. In ancient times, a crown was also a symbol of royalty, but it had a much broader use than that. Crowns—coronets and wreaths called *coronae*—represented all kinds of distinctions. They were awarded to honor high achievement in many fields: political, athletic, and military.

Greeks and Romans sometimes bestowed golden crowns, but most often these *coronae* were formed of vines and leaves. In the Greek Pan-Hellenic games, the original prizes to the victors were made of olive leaves, pine needles, or even wild celery. Can you imagine today's

Olympic athletes being excited about such a crown?

Throughout history there have been all sorts of crowns: crowns for beauty and crowns for achievement, crowns fairly won and crowns obtained by dishonesty and corruption.

You see, it's all about being #1. Human ambition—the inner drive to obtain a "crown"—has not changed since time began. We all desire to achieve some kind of recognition, and that desire is driven by needs for respect, approval, wealth, and/or power.

What do you desire the most? To own the newest gadget or the hottest car? To be known as a shrewd business person? To be admired for your physical appearance? To win the trophy for best athlete? To have others say, "You're the best mom/dad I know"? All of these "crowns" make us feel good, but when you get right down to it, they take root in the soil of pride—to be the best, above all others.

No wonder our eyebrows raise when we hear about a truly heroic action, motivated by courage and self-sacrifice. Something that truly *deserves* a crown of highest honor.

In ancient times, the wreath conveying the greatest honor was the *corona obsidionalis*. It was similar to our American Medal of Honor. Unlike other awards for noteworthy achievement, the *corona obsidionalis* was always presented on the battlefield, where the heroic action occurred. So it was always made from whatever grew on the field of battle: vines, grass, weeds, etc. It was awarded to the officer who saved a besieged army from destruction. To someone who delivered many soldiers from certain capture or death. To someone who turned defeat into victory, a cursed situation into a cause for blessing.

The *corona obsidionalis* was the most treasured crown of all. And it would play a pivotal role in reversing the choices that the first man and woman made in the Garden of Eden, our very first home....

WHY A GARDEN?

*What place is your heart
longing for—and why?*

Now the Lord God had planted a garden in the east,
in Eden; and there he put the man he had formed.
And the Lord God made all kinds of trees grow
out of the ground—trees that were pleasing
to the eye and good for food.
In the middle of the garden were the tree of life
and the tree of the knowledge of good and evil.
A river watering the garden flowed from Eden.

—GENESIS 2:8-10

A GLIMPSE OF PARADISE

My mother's parents were Irish. Pop's middle name was Riley. My grandmother, Rachel, had curly red hair and fair skin best suited to the cool, rainy weather of western Ireland.

Tea and a good book in front of a peat fire, fields glistening in a thousand different shades of green, sun breaking through the clouds to fall in patches on the hills, a garden brimming with flowers in the summer—these were images of home to them, though they lived out their lives in America.

I grew up in the thick, colorless, winter fogs and the dry, furnace-blast summers of central California. Though my father carried the unmistakable features of his Jewish forebears, the DNA of centuries in Galway was passed along to me through my mother. My hair is curly and red, my skin dangerously fair, and not at all suited to harsh sun.

When Brock and I traveled to Ireland for the first time many years ago, my pale complexion and curly hair seemed to wake up and say, "Hey! This is really great! I remember this! *Home!*"

Just as each of us is the physical product of generations of DNA passed on through our parents, we also are a product of spiritual DNA. The longing in our spirits for a place of beauty and peace can be traced back to spiritual DNA created in the perfect garden of man's first home.

> The Lord God took the man
> and put him in the Garden of Eden
> to cultivate it and keep it.
> —GENESIS 2:15, NASB

Did God say man was meant "to cultivate it and keep it"? Wow! What a gift! What a magnificent occupation!

As we admire the majestic redwoods of California or sit beside a lovely waterfall in Hawaii, there's no doubt there's something in our spiritual DNA that Adam and Eve passed along! Nature calls to us. It announces the presence of a great Creator. And it makes our souls long for a perfect world. Such beauty compels our hearts to glimpse what the paradise of Adam and Eve must have been like.

"Home!" we joke and say we're never going back to the real world. But *is* it a joke? Eden is what we're all still searching for, isn't it? That perfect garden, created by a loving God, *for us*! Every day our spiritual DNA reminds us that God did not originally create us to live in a life overgrown with the thorns of sorrow and suffering!

The Lord's intention for our lives was far different. David, the shepherd who became king, described it well:

> When I consider your heavens,
>   the work of your fingers,
> the moon and the stars,
>   which you have set in place,
> what is man that you are mindful of him,
>   the son of man that you care for him?

> You made him a little lower than the heavenly beings
>   and crowned him with glory and honor.
> You made him ruler over the works of your hands;
>   you put everything under his feet.
>
> —PSALM 8:3-6

Before the Fall, mankind's first parents wore crowns of glory and majesty in Paradise. They ruled together over the perfect creation of the King of heaven and earth. They had a personal, face-to-face, relationship with their Creator-King. We are told in Genesis 3:8-10 that the Lord Himself walked in the garden with them.

What must that have been like?

Picture yourself living in the most beautiful place you can imagine—with waterfalls, lush greenery, trees with fruit perfectly ripe for picking and eating. Imagine carrying on a face-to-face conversation with Jesus on a daily basis. What if you brought the King of heaven and earth gifts from the garden you personally cultivated?

Whenever Adam and Eve wanted to, they

could speak to the Lord, and He would answer back in an audible voice. What a glorious relationship they had with Him every day! They were not ruled by fear. They were ruled by God's love.

Adam and Eve lived for, perhaps, unrecorded ages in Eden's perfect environment and freely took from the Lord's overflowing abundance. Beyond the days of creation, there is no record of how long they lived in Eden. But oh, how lovely it must have been!

WHY THE THORNS?

What happened to our first idyllic home—
and why does that event still impact us today?

The woman said to the serpent,
"We may eat fruit from the trees in the garden,
but God did say,
'You must not eat fruit from the tree
that is in the middle of the garden,
and you must not touch it, or you will die.'"
"You will not surely die,"
the serpent said to the woman.
"For God knows that when you eat of it
your eyes will be opened,
and you will be like God, knowing good and evil."
—GENESIS 3:2-5

A VISION OF EDEN
AND THE ONE CHOICE THAT RUINED EVERYTHING

It was the first time Brock and I and our teenagers, Rachel, Jake, and Luke, drove the crooked little road to Hana on the Hawaiian island of Maui. The wonders of the drive made my imagination leap. To me, it was like entering the Garden of Eden.

Waterfalls cascaded off high pinnacles and plunged into clear, ice-cold pools, surrounded by tropical flowers. Was there ever any place so beautiful in all the earth, we wondered? At a bend in the road we gasped at the sight of a rainbow, which seemed to be blooming in the center of a thousand-foot fountain.

"This place is proof," I told Rachel, repeating what my mother once said to me, "that God never meant for there to be thorns in His creation."

"Far enough," Brock declared, parking the car along the narrow shoulder.

Our kids tumbled out and raced ahead to

the deserted swimming hole just up the path. Brock and I spread our woven mats on a boulder nearby and unpacked a lavish picnic. Wild chickens clucked in the underbrush as we picked wild bananas and guava from the trees.

Brock, yielding to his hunter instinct, said, "A man would have to be a fool to go hungry here. It's sort of like Eden, eh?"

Fourteen-year-old Luke grinned. "This is like Swiss Family Robinson. I'm gonna build myself a tree house, and I'm never going back."

Jake, two years older and wiser, replied, "Yeah. Just one problem. No girls."

Brock laughed. "Sounds like what Adam said to the Lord. 'Something's missing here, God.'" Brock put his arm around me. "I got my gal. So your mom and I will just stay here. You kids can go back, out into the world, find yourselves mates, and come back for a visit!"

It was one of those perfect days; so perfect it remains fresh in our memories no matter how many years pass. It was an Edenic vision. Something like what heaven might be.

The place our hearts long for. A place where anything needed is within reach.

The Garden of Eden was beautiful—so beautiful. Peaceful, nourishing, inviting, idyllic. A place where humans could walk in perfect friendship with God. There was no separation, no fear, only love.

It was a world without thorns.

But, as we well know from our world today, things didn't remain in that perfect condition. So what happened?

Our first parents were given everything they needed for perfect happiness, including each other. What's more, obeying God wasn't difficult. There was only one command: "You must not eat from the tree of the knowledge of good and evil" (Genesis 3:17).

Imagine! Obedience to *one* command stood between the idyllic world the Lord had made and devastation!

But the simplicity and beauty of this system—remembering only one "no"—wasn't enough to keep the first man and woman from giving in to temptation and falling into sin. God had given them full reign over any of the other trees in the Garden (Genesis 3:16). All they had to do was leave the *one* tree alone.

GREAT CONSEQUENCES— FOR THEM AND FOR US

Adam and Eve didn't leave the tree alone. The temptation was too great, and they fell for the crafty serpent's words. The consequences of that Fall were horrific!

> And the Lord God said, "The man has now become like one of us, knowing good and evil. He must not be allowed to reach out his hand and take also from the tree of life and eat, and live forever."
>
> —GENESIS 3:22

So Death entered the world where once there had been only Life and beauty.

Nor was immortality all that was lost. Adam and Eve also lost their perfect fellowship with God. And they lost their garden home:

> So the Lord God banished him (Adam) from the Garden of Eden to work the ground from which he had been taken. After he drove the

man out, he placed on the east side of the Garden of Eden cherubim and a flaming sword flashing back and forth to guard the way to the tree of life.

—Genesis 3:23-24

The serpent, the deceiver, was cursed. Eve was cursed. Adam was cursed. And the very earth was cursed:

To Adam he said, "Because you listened to your wife and ate from the tree about which I commanded you, 'You must not eat of it,'

"Cursed is the ground because of you;
  through painful toil you will eat of it
  all the days of your life.
It will produce *thorns* and thistles for you."

—Genesis 3:17-18

Because Adam and Eve chose to disregard God's warning and yielded to Satan's temptation to eat of the fruit of the tree so they could be "like God," they threw away every good thing God had created for them.

The Hebrew word for "overflowing abundance" is *ShePHA*. Rearrange the same Hebrew letters, and the word becomes *PeShA*, "rebellious sin."

In an act of pride, Adam and Eve rearranged the letters of God's creation.

They exchanged the overflowing abundance of Eden and their relationship with their Creator for sinful rebellion against the Lord's Kingship over their lives.

Because of their rebellion, they exchanged Life for Death. They threw away the crowns of glory and majesty and exchanged them for desolation and sorrow. And because of their choice, a forgotten grave, overgrown by thorns, became the ultimate, inevitable end of every life. Thus thorns became a symbol of the result of sin.

Because we are the children of Adam and Eve, we also find ourselves in the same sinful, fallen state. We too have been banished from perfect friendship with God because of our sin. One of the symptoms of this separation is the amount of stress and worry we attach to *things* in this life. How often such anxiety causes indifference to the things of God!

Jesus Himself confirmed this in the Parable of the Sower in Matthew 13:1-23, in which He compares the Word of God to seed being scattered by a farmer. In verse 7 He says, "Other seed fell among thorns, which grew up and choked the plants."

Later, when His disciples asked for an explanation of His teaching, Jesus elaborated in verse 22: "The one who received the seed that fell among the thorns is the man who hears the word, but the worries of this life and the deceitfulness of wealth choke it, making it unfruitful."

Do you often feel that way—unfruitful? Do the concerns of life weigh you down, choking out your concern for the things of God?

All of creation suffered because of the disobedience of Adam and Eve. Outside the garden of God's perfect fellowship and loving care, thorns grew up and took over the earth. Those thorns of sin have entangled every man and woman born since that moment.

WHY A WAR?

*Why is there so much pain and suffering
in the world—and in my life?*

Crown Him the Son of God,
before the worlds began,
And ye who tread where He hath trod,
crown Him the Son of Man;
Who every grief hath known
that wrings the human breast,
And takes and bears them for His own,
that all in Him may rest.

—"CROWN HIM WITH MANY CROWNS"
VERSE 3, WORDS BY GODFREY THRING, 1874

DRIVEN OUT!

After living unrecorded ages in the beauty and overflowing abundance of Eden, what must it have been like for Adam and Eve to have been driven out by the Lord?

Suddenly they found themselves alone in a wilderness, where thorns choked the desolate earth. Hunger, thirst, cold, and searing heat must have been a shock to them as they looked back at the abundance they had given up through rebellion.

But rather than turn back to God, their Maker, they continued in their rebellion. They complicated an already bad situation further by their actions. The first human death ever recorded was an act of murder. Out of jealousy, Adam and Eve's first son, Cain, murdered his younger brother, Abel (Genesis 4:1-14). What an unbearable grief it must have been to the first parents when they realized that their firstborn son had acted out the terrible consequence of their own yielding to sin: "for when you eat of it you will surely die" (Genesis 2:17).

Brothers have been fighting one another for position and approval and authority ever since. And the results have been horrific.

THE WAR TO END ALL WARS

I was only seven in August, 1957, when my grandmother gave me the little pocket edition New Testament my grandfather carried when he fought in the trenches of France in World War I. I did not realize it at the time, but the date she inscribed it to me marked the twelfth anniversary of Pop's death.

We sat on the back porch that night as she told me how, at hearing the news the fighting was over, she climbed onto a fire wagon to ride with a hundred other people up and down the streets of Akron, celebrating all night. She banged two pots together and whooped for joy until she lost her voice. There had never been a war like that one. So many young men did not come home. But lots of prayers and the Bible in Pop's rucksack kept him safe, she said.

I was grown before I realized just how terrible Pop's war had been. It was called "The War to End All Wars." Never before in all of history had so many men died in battle. Combine a thousand years of war, and the death toll does not add up to the casualties of that one conflagration.

World War I could also be called "The War of Crowns," because of what happened "behind the scenes." Over sixty crowned heads of Europe were all cousins, each tracing their lineage back to Queen Victoria of England. King George V of England was cousin to his enemy, Kaiser Wilhelm of Germany, and also cousin to Czar Nicholas of Russia. Beginning with these three kings in 1914, the world was thrown into a savage conflict that would not end until millions had died. And this enormous royal family feud, "The War to End All Wars," was just the *beginning* of a century of horrors.

Pop's diary told of what he faced in the

trenches of France. Sixty years later we re-counted some of the details of his story through the eyes of Birch Tucker in the novel, *In My Father's House.*

In World War 1, poison gas and mechanized warfare guaranteed the deaths of millions of ordinary men who had dreamed of much longer futures…men who had longed for a better life and a just, safe world for their loved ones.

Today, once again, we are plunged into warfare. As we bury dear sons and daughters who die fighting against tyranny around the world, our grieving hearts cry out for justice. "O, Lord! Open the gates and let the King of Righteousness come in!"

But who is this King of Righteousness we long for? The One our souls cry out for? Who is the only One fit to wear the greatest of all crowns? The only One fit to rule over our lives and hearts in justice and mercy and unfailing love?

Who in all heaven and earth is worthy to

wear a crown inscribed with the words, *Holy Unto the Lord?*

WHY A SOLDIER?

*Did you know that every day
you are part of a great battle?*

Onward Christian soldiers, marching as to war,
With the cross of Jesus going on before.
Christ, the royal Master, leads against the foe;
Forward into battle see His banners go!

Crowns and thrones may perish, kingdoms rise and wane,
But the church of Jesus constant will remain.
Gates of hell can never 'gainst that church prevail;
We have Christ's own promise, and that cannot fail.

—"ONWARD, CHRISTIAN SOLDIERS"
WORDS BY SABINE BARING-GOULD, 1865

THE FIGHT OF YOUR LIFE

Great battles and wars are not only fought between mighty nations. Every day we are soldiers in a war against pride, hatred, selfish ambition, immorality, idolatry, factions, envy, jealousy, fits of rage, hopelessness, fear, worry, and disappointment with God.

God never intended your life to be full of thorns. You are not created to wound others or to be wounded. But each day we come to the end of our day more bloody and weary than we were the day before.

"Abundant life? Not in this world!" we cry.

Yet Jesus said it! He told us straight out why He left heaven to live among us! "I have come that they may have life, and have it to the full" (John 10:10). Life to the full! *Abundant Life!*

What are the signs of this *Abundant Life* Jesus came to give us? Galatians 5:22-23 defines what we are created to experience: "But the fruit of the Spirit is love, joy, peace, patience, kindness, goodness, faithfulness, gentleness and self-control."

Is your life filled with love?

Do you wake up each morning with a sense of joy and excitement about what the day has in store for you?

Do you lay your head on your pillow to sleep at night with an overwhelming feeling of peace in spite of your circumstances?

Do you have patience when your prayers are not answered as you wish, or as soon as you wanted?

Do you demonstrate kindness when someone is not kind to you?

Do you show gentleness in the midst of disagreements?

Do you display self-control as you drive down the freeway and someone cuts you off?

Or have you lost all hope that your life can ever be filled with "love, joy, peace, patience, kindness, goodness, faithfulness, gentleness and self-control"?

These are the issues *our* battles are made of! These are the thorns that choke out our lives in a million little ways.

THE ONLY PERFECT PERSON

God was right to drive Adam and Eve out of Eden when He did. After darkness and pride and rage took control of the hearts of mankind, we would have torn God's perfect garden to pieces.

So the first Adam was driven out. And we, his descendants, have been searching for a way back home ever since!

But in all the long, tortured history of man on earth, only one has ever lived in a way that completely demonstrated all the perfect qualities of a life without sin.

That person was Jesus!

The second Adam, God's dear Son, *voluntarily* left the Eden that is heaven to search for us among the thorns of earth. He fought the battle we were losing and He *won!*

But how could He do it, when our first parents, Adam and Eve, failed?

WHY A SACRIFICE?

What if someone was willing
to trade places with you?
To pay the price
for everything you've done wrong?

What Thou, my Lord, has suffered,
Was all for sinners' gain;
Mine, mine was the transgression,
But Thine the deadly pain.

—"O SACRED HEAD, NOW WOUNDED"
WORDS ATTRIBUTED TO BERNARD OF CLAIRVAUX, 1153

A WILLING SUBSTITUTE?!

Abraham was a man who made many bad choices—and also experienced many miracles. When he was a hundred years old, his barren, ninety-year-old wife bore her first child, a son. They were overjoyed! At last, they had an heir…the start of a great nation, as God had promised.

But God chose to test Abraham, to see if his faith in God was solid. God asked him to sacrifice his only son, Isaac—Abraham's pride and joy. Isaac, the only hope for the future of Abraham's family. The story is told in Genesis, chapter 22.

Why would God demand such a sacrifice? Because God knew it was the only way to test Abraham's heart. Would Abraham choose to obey God, no matter what? Or would he choose his own way?

Abraham, broken-hearted, anguished, followed God's direction.

And God answered.

Just as Abraham raised the knife to kill his son, God intervened. An angel called out, "Abraham! Abraham!...Do not lay a hand on the boy....Do not do anything to him. Now I know that you fear God, because you have not withheld from me your son, your only son" (verses 11-12).

But that's not the end of the story: "Abraham looked up and there in a thicket he saw a ram caught by its horns. He went over and took the ram and sacrificed it as a burnt offering instead of his son" (verse 13).

In other words, the tale of Abraham's obedient faith and Isaac's rescue does not end without a sacrifice. The ram ensnared in the thorns became the substitute for the life of the boy. The ram was not a willing sacrifice, however. He was ensnared in the thorns and unable to escape.

Why do we bring up this tale now?

Because Jesus was a *willing* sacrifice for you and me!

Here's what happened when Jesus was arrested:

The men stepped forward, seized Jesus, and arrested him. With that, one of Jesus' companions reached for his sword, drew it out and struck the servant of the high priest, cutting off his ear.

"Put your sword back in its place," Jesus said to him, "for all who draw the sword will die by the sword. Do you think I cannot call on my Father, and he will at once put at my disposal more than twelve legions of angels? But how then would the Scriptures be fulfilled that say it must happen in this way?"

—MATTHEW 26:50-54

And listen to what Jesus taught:

"I am the good shepherd. The good shepherd lays down his life for the sheep.... No one takes it from me, but I lay it down of my own accord. I have authority to lay it down and authority to take it up again. This command I received from my Father."

—JOHN 10:11,18

Do you hear what Jesus says? He has the authority, the Crown, to willingly lay down His life to be the substitute sacrifice for you. And, as He proved at the Resurrection (John 20), He did indeed have the authority to take it up again.

Jesus paid the sacrifice for our sins when He died on the cross (John 19:16-30)!

Now, why is that important to us?

Because not only did Jesus *willingly* take our punishment and receive our death sentence, His death and resurrection is the *down payment* on what He intends to give us—Eternal Life! (1 Corinthians 15:1-23).

Listen to what Jesus promises to those who love Him and keep His commandments:

"Be faithful, even to the point of death, and I will give you the crown of life."

—Revelation 2:10

The crown of life is an award of life that surpasses all others. It's a recognition that the Life Jesus offers us is the highest quality and of unlimited duration!

There's only one catch to it.

WHY ONLY ONE KING?

*If only one person was in charge
of your life, should it be you?*

The devil took him to a very high mountain
and showed him all the kingdoms of the world
and their splendor.
"All this I will give you," he said,
"If you will bow down and worship me."
Jesus said to him, "Away from me, Satan!
For it is written: 'Worship the Lord your God,
And serve him only.'"
—MATTHEW 4:8-10

LIKE GOD?

When Adam and Eve lived in the perfect environment of Eden, they experienced the literal nearness and a face-to-face fellowship with the Lord. But who exactly was this Lord?

Scripture tells us it was Jesus—in His pre-incarnate form! Jesus has always existed and, by His word, created the heavens and the earth and all that is in them.

> In the beginning was the Word, and the Word was with God, and the Word was God. He was with God in the beginning.
>
> Through him all things were made...In him was life, and that life was the light of men.
>
> —JOHN 1:1-4

But the sweet purity of Adam and Eve's relationship with their Maker was ruined when Adam and Eve disobeyed. When they decided to be "like God." In essence, they made a choice to be king and queen of their own lives, rather than choosing to let

God rule.

We each have followed in Adam's footsteps. Romans 3:23 says, "For all have sinned and fall short of the glory of God." Every day we choose to follow our own path rather than God's path for us. The result is always disaster!

Take a look at your own personal history. What wrong choices have you made in life? What do you wish you had done differently? Just looking back at a few of those choices is proof that God makes a much better ruler over our lives than we do!

In the constant daily struggle of life's temptations and conflicts, who of us has not said, "I do not understand what I do. For what I want to do I do not do, but what I hate I do" (Romans 7:15)?

Who of us has not cried, "What a wretched man I am! Who will rescue me from this body of death?" (Romans 7:24).

No wonder our hearts long so desperately for the King of Righteousness to rule over our broken lives in mercy and restore us to the perfection of Eden! Where we can, like the first parents, walk and talk with our Maker.

Where is the One who is worthy to wear the Crown of eternal Kingship and rule over your heart?

Only Jesus is the ultimate Victor over all the thorns of temptation and failures that we fight against. Only He can return our hearts to the joy and peace of Eden. And it's all part of a master plan.

WHY A PLAN?

What if you thought about your troubles
and sins as already redeemed?
How would that affect your life now—
and for all eternity?

Therefore, there is now no condemnation
for those who are in Christ Jesus,
because through Christ Jesus
the law of the Spirit of life set me free
from the law of sin and death.

—ROMANS 8:1-2

A BATTLE DECLARATION

From the beginning God set in motion a plan to redeem us. He spelled out his battle plan to the enemy when He cursed Satan after the temptation of Eve:

"Because you have done this,
     cursed are you....
And I will put enmity
     between you and the woman,
     and between your offspring and hers;
he will crush your head,
     and you will strike his heel."

—Genesis 3:14-15

By those words, God clearly announced to Satan, "There will be a great conflict between you, the Prince of Darkness, and the Anointed One, the Messiah, King of Righteousness."

In that opening declaration of war, God showed Satan that he was doomed to lose

the war for our souls! After all, though the
Messiah may be wounded on the heel, that's
not a fatal wound. But a crushing blow to
the serpent's head *is* a fatal wound.

More of the mystery is revealed in Scripture. How exactly would this Messiah enter
the plan to redeem all of mankind?

> But when the time had fully come, God
> sent his Son, born of a woman, born under
> law, to redeem those under law, that we might
> receive the full rights of sons. Because you
> are sons, God sent the Spirit of his Son
> into our hearts, the Spirit who calls out,
> "*Abba,* (Papa!) Father."
>
> —GALATIANS 4:4-6

Who exactly was this Son of God who
walked the earth? All who heard Jesus'
message or saw his miracles wondered. Some
believed he was of God. Others believed
he was just a good man. Our novel, *Third
Watch,* explores this vital question....

Jesus of Nazareth tossed out the question one evening as He camped with His disciples near the spring where the river was born. His disciples sat around the fire roasting quail on sticks for supper. Their shadows loomed against the rock face. An owl hooted from a tree outside their circle. Smoke stung Matthew's eyes. John stirred the embers.

"What are the rumors then?" Jesus asked. "Tell me. Who do men say that I am?"

His disciples were so used to Him by then that they hardly glanced up from the flames as they replied, "No one knows for sure who you are. Prophet. Liar. Lawgiver. Rebel. Rabbi. Heretic. Good Man. Bad Man."

Such bland, insignificant definitions were like shadows on the rocks. No substance. No strength. After all, it took no commitment to call Jesus "a good man."

But upon His *next* question the gates of eternity hinged. "Who do *you* say that I am?"

It was Simon who blurted out the answer around a mouthful of quail meat. Simon, licking his fingers, who spoke the truth straight-out and got it right on the first try. This surprised everyone, including Simon.

"Who do *you* say that I am?..."

Simon was a fisherman, not a poet. He said what he said so plainly that it seemed as if he believed it. But Simon did not believe it. Not really. Or at least he could not comprehend the complexity and significance of what he had just declared.

Perhaps at the time no one could comprehend what Simon's answer truly meant. No one. Not yet.

Even now, after everything, the vastness of Jesus' identity and what He holds in His hand is impossible for the human mind to grasp.

He is
the One who knows the beginning
and the midpoint and the end of times.
He knows
the force of the elements,
the organization of the universe,

cycles of seasons and years,
position of stars,
personalities of men and beasts,
powers of winds and thoughts of all men.

It is written that an hour is coming when every knee will bow and every tongue confess that Jesus, the Messiah, is Adonai, the Lord.

For every soul that moment will come.

Look! Jesus approaches the shore and calls out The Question! You do not answer Him, yet the boat draws nearer. Its keel scrapes onto the sand. He steps into the water, wades to shore, takes your hand, looks you in the eyes and asks: "Who do you say that I am?"

Eternal destiny depends on the answer. You know the truth. Oh, yes. There's no denying it now. You know.

No excuses. Not like before.

But there was a time when Jesus lived on earth among men and the only creatures who recognized Him were those fallen angels cast out of heaven with the Great Deceiver to rule this world. Demons possessed men, dwelt within mortal bodies, and held them in bondage. Controlling the human mind, they whispered lies and fear and hopelessness and rebellion and suicide to their human hosts. They peered out at the world through human eyes. They committed adultery, stole, cheated, and murdered with human hands. They lied, boasted, gossiped, slandered, and blasphemed with human tongues.

And then The Light came to earth as the prophets foretold in Holy Scripture. Born as a man named Jesus, which means "Salvation," He lived among us.

The Angel of the Lord. El Shaddai. Adonai. The Way. The Truth. The Life. The Living Word of God. Savior. Messiah. Redeemer. The Anointed One. El Olam. Ancient of Days.

So many names of grace and beauty to call Him—as many names as there are human needs to meet. And so The One Lord of All Eternity came to our world to ask each heart The One Question: *Who do* you *say I am?*

This is the story of the battle between The Truth and the Father of Lies. Each fought mightily for the souls of mankind.

Those who witnessed the conflict firsthand could not comprehend how ancient this war was, nor what the outcome meant for generations yet to be born.

—*THIRD WATCH*

Think of what Jesus gave up to come and personally fight the final battle in the war between Satan and God over the souls of mankind. Over your soul—and mine!

The apostle Paul, writing while he was in a battle for his own life (awaiting trial on an appeal to the Roman emperor Nero), explained the earthly mission of Jesus in Philippians 2:5-11:

Your attitude should be the same as that of
Christ Jesus:
Who, being in very nature God,
   did not consider equality with God
   something to be grasped,
but made himself nothing,
   taking the very nature of a servant,
   being made in human likeness.
And being found in appearance as a man,
   he humbled himself
   and became obedient to death—
   even death on a cross!
Therefore God exalted him to the highest place
   and gave him the name that is above every name,

that at the name of Jesus every knee should bow,
   in heaven and on earth and under the earth,
and every tongue confess that Jesus Christ is Lord,
   to the glory of God the Father.

Jesus' first mission on earth was certainly not what anyone expected!

If you were one of his disciples around the campfire, roasting your dinner on a stick and talking with Jesus, how would you have answered his question, "Who do *you* say that I am?"

WHY A WOUNDED MESSIAH?

*Why would the King of all leave heaven
to lay down His life?*

Crown Him the Lord of love,
behold His hands and side,
Rich wounds, yet visible above,
in beauty glorified.
No angel in the sky
can fully bear that sight,
But downward bends his burning eye
at mysteries so bright.

—"CROWN HIM WITH MANY CROWNS"
VERSE 6, WORDS BY MATTHEW BRIDGES, 1852

CROWN HIM WITH MANY CROWNS . . .

The Messiah of Israel, expected to be descended from King David, would be entitled to wear the crown of David (Jeremiah 23:5; 33:15). As the ultimate fulfillment of the promises made to King David, Jesus of Nazareth was entitled to David's throne.

But that's not the only authority Messiah was expected to have. Messiah was also said to be:

*The Redeemer of Israel (Isaiah 49:7)
*The Light of the Gentiles (Isaiah 60:3)
*The King of Glory (Psalm 24:7-10)

He would be the fulfillment of God's promises to Abraham about how through Abraham all the nations of the world would be blessed (Genesis 18:18; 22:18).

He would be crowned highest and best in all these areas: Wonderful Counselor, Mighty God, Everlasting Father, Prince of Peace (Isaiah 9:6-7).

He would be God With Us—Immanuel (Isaiah 7:14).

Each of these titles are like crowns, representing either a virtue that only Messiah would possess to the highest possible degree, or a title acknowledging that only Messiah can fulfill one of the promises of God to His people.

But the prophetic statements about Messiah are not universally about honor and acclaim. There's a darker side too.

> He was pierced for our transgressions,
>   he was crushed for our iniquities;
> the punishment that brought us
>   peace was upon him,
>   and by his wounds we are healed.
>
> —ISAIAH 53:5

How can two total opposite reactions both be true? Why was Immanuel—God With Us—"pierced," "crushed," "punished," and "wounded"?

In our novel *First Light*, we imagined Jesus revealing the "why" to the shepherd Zadok, who suffered much for his belief in Messiah....

"The penalty for breaking the commands of the Almighty," Jesus told Zadok, "is death. That curse now rests on every human soul. Redemption costs something, Zadok, my old friend."

Zadok leaned close. Firelight glowed golden on his face. "But can the cost of our salvation be so high?"

"Tomorrow I'll be teaching in Beth-Anyah."

"So close to Jerusalem! You'll draw the wolves out along with the sheep. You put yourself at their mercy."

"A day is coming when they will understand God's Mercy."

"But not that way, Lord! Tell me it won't be!"

"God's love for each person is that profound."

"There must be another way! Crush our enemies! Call down fire from heaven! Destroy the wicked! Set up a kingdom in Jerusalem like our shepherd-king, David! Like you, he was born here in Beth-lehem!"

"Zadok, when the soldiers of Herod came to Beth-lehem to kill every baby boy, you sought to save your three sons." Jesus touched the scar on Zadok's cheek. "This scar is proof of your love for your children."

"I failed. I am alive and my babies are in their graves."

"Not for want of effort. You would have died to save your little ones. I know you. Even now you'd face a lion and lay down your life to save your flocks. Can the Son sent by the Father do any less for the flock given to him? Would you deny the Lord the honor of wounds and scars that will be eternal proof of how much he loves you?"

"I will die for you, Lord."

"He was led like a lamb to slaughter."

"But I am more ready to give up my own life! Gladly!"

"One day it may be so. Anyone who lays down his life for my sake will find it. God so loved the world that whoever believes in his Son will never die but will inherit eternal life. But first, the good shepherd will lay down his life to save his flock. That price must be paid to redeem those the Father has given to me. The prophecy of what will happen is all there, recorded by Moses and the prophets. They longed to see what you see, to hear what you have heard. The battle for mankind will be won."

"Rabbi, will we fight the enemy then? Together?"

"Don't misunderstand, old friend...*by his wounds we are healed.*"

Shoulders sagged. With a groan Zadok bowed his head. Ran crooked fingers through his thatch of white hair. "Ah! No! And after such a fine beginnin'. I looked up! Saw the stars shinin' there above us in the field. Such joy we felt. What a beautiful baby boy! Such hope! What's it for? It can't be meant to end so ill!"

Silence descended. Then, finally, Jesus replied, "It can't be any other way."

—*First Light*

The first Adam was expelled from Eden because he chose sin over the company of the Lord.

The second Adam chose to leave the perfection and peace of heaven in search of all the lost children of Adam! Jesus, the King and Creator, reached up and removed His crown of glory from His sacred head. He laid aside all His mighty power and left heaven to enter the world of thorns and heartache. He lived without sin, without drawing on His own Eternal power, but by complete dependence on the guidance and strength and authority of the Holy Spirit.

Jesus, who was Lord of all the Angel Armies, went into battle against the Prince of Darkness without a physical sword. The King of Righteousness, Holy Unto the Lord, wore no priestly vestments. The King of Heaven and Earth was not dressed as a King.

When Satan taunted Him, saying, "All this I will give you if you will bow down and worship *me!*" Jesus' defense was to quote the absolute truth of God's Holy Word back to the Evil One. And with this weapon, Jesus thwarted the Prince of Darkness!

Satan had claimed the souls of all mankind and the world on the day the first Adam and his wife yielded to the temptation to become "like God."

Jesus, the second Adam, began the reclamation of mankind for eternity when He faced off with Satan in the wilderness and used Scripture as His defense.

Today He offers you that same power. All you have to do is use it.

WHY THE MOCKING?

They made fun of him on purpose,
but could that mocking also be
part of heaven's grand plan?

Then the governor's soldiers took Jesus into the
Praetorium and gathered the whole company of
soldiers around him. They stripped him and put
a scarlet robe on him, and then twisted together a
crown of thorns and set it on his head. They put a
staff in his right hand and knelt in front of him and
mocked him. "Hail, king of the Jews!" they said.
They spit on him and took the staff and struck him
on the head again and again. After they had mocked
him, they took off the robe and put his own clothes
on him. Then they led him away to crucify him.

—MATTHEW 27:27-31

"THIS IS THE KING OF THE JEWS"

The torture inflicted on Jesus by the Roman soldiers in their cruel game with the crown of thorns and the mockery is significant enough that three of the four Gospel writers record the incident. (Only Luke omits this detail, while still recording that "The soldiers made fun of Jesus....")

All four Gospels mention the fact that Governor Pilate caused a sign to be written and placed on the cross over Jesus' head: "This is the King of the Jews." It was common practice for condemned criminals to have their crimes posted at their execution.

The religious leaders had charged Jesus with blasphemy, for which the punishment was death by stoning. But because they had a very limited right to inflict capital punishment, they wanted to be certain that Pilate shared in this abuse of power.

Pilate said he found no fault in Jesus but

agreed to the execution because he was afraid of the people (and their threat to send complaints to Caesar). So it was decided that Jesus would die for the Roman crime of treason, and the sentence would be the Roman punishment of death on the cross.

There were two reasons for Pilate's sign.

First, by asserting Jesus' claim to be King of the Jews, Pilate justified his own actions. No one could be King of the Jews without the approval of Rome, and no unauthorized person could claim to be King of the Jews without being guilty of treason against Rome. And rebellion against Rome was punished by death.

Second, nailing up the sign was a warning to any in the crowd who might dare to hope that a messiah would come to free Judea from the Romans. The not-so-subtle message was, *Here's what happens to anyone who claims to be the King of the Jews...take notice and beware!*

How ironic it is that Pilate inadvertently gave Jesus His correct title! Jesus *was* and *is* the *only* true King of the Jews. Yet the one government official who stated that fact did it while presiding over Jesus' execution!

Even the mocking sign at Jesus' death on the cross continued the ironic mistreatment of his scornful abuse begun at the hands of the soldiers.

And the torment and ridicule combined to fulfill prophetic utterances about what Messiah would suffer: "All who see me mock me; they hurl insults, shaking their heads" (Psalm 22:7).

All was a part of the grand plan...from the very beginning.

WHY THE
CROWN OF SIN?

*Who would claim the title
of Greatest Sinner of All?*

I love Thee because Thou has first loved me,
And purchased my pardon on Calvary's tree.
I love Thee for wearing the thorns on Thy brow;
If ever I loved Thee, my Jesus, 'tis now.

—"MY JESUS, I LOVE THEE"
WORDS BY WILLIAM R. FEATHERSTON, 1864

WHAT CROWN *DID* JESUS RECEIVE?

There was a time when the people of Israel were excited to welcome Jesus as Messiah. He was healer, provider, comforter, counselor.

On the first day of the week before Jesus' final Passover celebration on earth, the citizens of Jerusalem welcomed Jesus with palm branches. They spread their cloaks on the ground for his donkey to tread upon (Matthew 21:1-11).

This was the welcome offered to an arriving hero, a conqueror, a head of state. And the Messiah!

The crowds exclaimed: "Hosanna to the son of David! Blessed is he who comes in the name of the Lord! Hosanna in the highest!"

If the crowds had possessed a gold crown, don't you think they would have offered it to Jesus right then?

Then, less than a week later, Jesus was dead—crucified—after having first been scorned, mocked, and crowned with thorns.

Thorns that represent the result of sin…a curse pronounced by God upon the earth.

Thorns that represent indifference to the things of God, inattention to the commands of God.

Thorns emblematic of unwillingness to obey the leading of God.

All these were braided together and forced down upon Jesus' head. He was given the crown—a mark of superiority the recognition due the person who was the greatest sinner in all the world.

Jesus received the Crown of Sin!

Imagine standing in a large, packed stadium. If the crowd was asked who thought they might be worthy of the distinction "Chief of Sinners," many of us (if we're honest) would, red-faced with guilt, raise our hands to claim the title.

The apostle Paul did. Listen to his words to young Timothy: "Here is a trustworthy saying that deserves full acceptance: Christ Jesus came into the world to save sinners—of whom I am the worst" (1 Timothy

1:15). Any others out there care to claim the title?

But NOT Jesus! The One who was awarded the crown of distinction, "Greatest Sinner of All," was the One who could not possibly deserve it!

Listen to what Peter says in his first letter: "He committed no sin, and no deceit was found in his mouth" (1 Peter 2:22).

Elsewhere Paul says it even more forcefully: "God made him to be sin for us, so that in him we might become the righteousness of God" (2 Corinthians 5:21).

Not only did Jesus take all of sin on Himself—our sins, your sins, the sins of the whole world. Not only did He receive the punishment for those sins. He was *made sin*. God looked at His own precious Son, Jesus, and saw all that was vile, treacherous, rebellious, and hateful.

And the Crown of Thorns represents that transformation, when all the putrid effects of our sin were heaped on the head of Jesus!

WHY THE *CORONA OBSIDIONALIS?*

*The great transformation:
suffering into glory?*

Thine shall the glory be;
Lest I forget Thy thorn crowned brow,
Lead me to Calvary.

—"LEAD ME TO CALVARY"

WORDS BY JENNIE E. HUSSEY, 1921

THE WRONG CROWN—
OR THE RIGHT ONE?

Cheering combat to the death between gladiators in the arena. Practicing perhaps the most horrific form of execution ever known.

Can there be any doubt that Romans could be both creative and deliberate in their cruelty?

Nowhere is this more evident than in the Roman soldiers' treatment of Jesus. Pilate's troopers may not have cared at all for politics or Jewish prophecy, but they certainly picked up on the opportunity to combine scorn with torture.

Besides carrying out whipping and beating, some legionary located and braided together the crown of thorns for the amusement of his friends. Add a purple robe, a fake scepter, and the crown of mockery—and the ridicule of an innocent man was complete.

So was the irony. Remember the curse laid on the ground after Adam and Eve sinned:

"It will produce thorns and thistles for you" (Genesis 3:18)?

Ever since man's initial indifference to the commands of God, the entire universe has awaited the coming of the One who could set things right (Romans 8:22). Not only someone who could receive the punishment for one other, or ten, or a thousand, but the One who could carry all the punishments for all the sins of all time. The One who could, at long last, redeem the whole earth from the curse!

Remember the *corona obsidionalis*? The highest award given in the ancient world to the One who saved an army from certain destruction, reversed the tide of battle, lifted the siege, and set a doomed population free? It was always woven from whatever grew on the field of battle—vines, weeds, even thorns!

Now see Jesus, the One, the Redeemer. The Savior who sets mankind free and redeems the whole of creation from the curse of sin. See Him at the moment of victory,

His death on the cross, being awarded exactly the most appropriate accolade possible—the *corona obsidionalis!*

Did the Roman soldiers, intent on scorning the King of the Jews, have that thought in mind as they pressed the barbs into Jesus' flesh? Not at all, but first-century believers, knowing the recorded curse, the Promised Redeemer, *and* the fulfillment at the cross of Calvary, could not have missed it.

The Crown of Scorn was, in fact, the Crown of Victory!

By laying down His life willingly and freely, Jesus filled up in Himself all the punishment for all the sins, for all the indifference to the things of God, and yes, even for all the mockery, down through all the centuries.

No wonder the writer of Hebrews says: "How shall we escape if we ignore such a great salvation?" and "But we see Jesus, who was made a little lower than the angels, now *crowned* with glory and honor because he suffered death, so that by the grace of God he might taste death for everyone" (2:3, 9).

IN THE GARDEN?

What will your last moments on earth be like?
Where will you spend eternity?

Let every tribe and every tongue
before Him prostrate fall
And shout in universal song
the crowned Lord of all.

—"ALL HAIL THE POWER OF JESUS' NAME"
WORDS BY EDWARD PERRONET, 1780

SPRING, 2005

The yellow roses in my mother's garden bloomed outside her bedroom window. I sat at her bedside, knowing that these were the last moments we would share together here on earth.

She held my hand as we prayed "The Lord's Prayer" and named every member of our family. We were silent a minute, then she squeezed my hand and, in a faint whisper, began to sing the old hymn.

I sang with her.

> "I come to the garden alone,
> while the dew is still on the roses
> and the voice I hear
> falling on my ear,
> the Son of God discloses . . .
> and He walks with me
> and He talks with me,
> and He tells me I am His own . . .
> and the joy we share as we tarry there
> none other has ever known…"

No second verse. It was enough for me to know....

Mama opened her clear, green eyes and smiled at me. "I'm going home now, Bodie. Home. Don't worry. His garden. Yellow roses. Oh, look! No thorns...I'll be there with Mom and Pop and...Jesus...waiting to hug you when you come home...."

Forty years had passed since Mama and I stood together before the cross near her Pop's grave. Forty years since she told me the crown of thorns really meant something. She knew that Jesus had come to wear the thorns of suffering, which had threatened to choke out the beauty of her life.

She spent her last forty years telling everyone she met: "Jesus loves you! Jesus died to win a great victory to save you! Never lose hope! Trust Him with your life, and He will give Eternal Life back to you! And until that great day, you can live life on this earth, healed, and whole, and filled with joy!"

I remember the joyful Christian life she lived. I remember her sweet song in the moments before she went to her Eternal home. I remember her smile of assurance that the place God created for us is a garden without thorns. It is a real place, where we can go because the battlefield crown of victory Jesus wore was the Crown of Thorns.

This story of sorrow, uprooted by joy, is forever engraved on my heart!

> This grace was given us in Christ Jesus before the beginning of time, but it has now been revealed through the appearing of our Savior, Christ Jesus, who has destroyed death and has brought life and immortality to light through the gospel.
>
> —2 TIMOTHY 1:9-10

IT'S ALL FOR YOU

The King of kings deserves
the proper place in your life.
He longs for it.

What can I give Him,
poor as I am.
If I were a shepherd,
I would bring a lamb.
If I were a Wise Man,
I would do my part.
But what I can, I give Him—
give my heart.
—Christina Rossetti, 1894

WHAT WILL YOU OFFER?

What crown have you offered to Jesus?

Some people are actively antagonistic toward God. They offer Jesus rebelliousness, anger, hostility, or bitterness.

Other individuals say, "I haven't done anything particularly bad or wrong. So I guess what I offer is 'Live and Let Live.' I may turn to God when I really need him, but not now. Not today."

Friend, did you know that indifference to the will of God is the same as rebellion, the same as offering Jesus another Crown of Thorns?

So what will *you* offer Him?

You possess the crown of authority over your own life and will. Jesus will never force Himself into your life. He waits to be invited. So why not step aside from being #1 in your life? When you think about it, have you really run things that well anyway? Don't you long for the confused elements of your existence to make sense? Don't you want to know for certain that Someone greater than yourself—the King of kings and Lord of lords—is in charge of the universe?

Don't wait! Do it today!

Your transformation awaits. All you need is a willing, humble heart to pray this simple prayer:

"Here's the crown of my life, Lord Jesus.
I surrender it to you. By an act of my will
I consciously want you to be
the authority in my life....not me."

Why not record this moment when your life changed for all eternity?

_____

my signature

_____

date

You can be assured that "If you seek Him, He will be found by you" (1 Chronicles 28:9)!

WHAT NEXT?

Because you have trusted your life to Jesus, the Redeemer, your sins are forgiven. You are born again, and the Lord promises you have Eternal Life!

You ask, "What do I do now?"

#1 Tell someone.
Tell a Christian friend *right now* that you have asked Jesus to come into your heart. Or email us: brockandbodie@littlebooksofwhy.com.
We'll celebrate with you and pray for you.

> Let us hold unswervingly to the hope we profess, for he who promised is faithful.
>
> —HEBREWS 10:23

#2 Read the Bible.
There is only one book you can trust above all others to give you the *truth* about Jesus —the Bible. If any book disagrees with these God-breathed words, it is *not* the truth. Begin by reading the Gospel of John. There are many modern translations that will make the story even more understandable.

All Scripture is God-breathed and is useful for teaching, rebuking, correcting and training in righteousness, so that the man of God may be thoroughly equipped for every good work.

—2 TIMOTHY 3:16

#3 Find fellowship.
Find a Bible-believing church where you can experience joy, fellowship, and learn about God's Word. Ask to be baptized (Galatians 3:25-27).

Let us not give up meeting together...
but let us encourage one another.

—HEBREWS 10:25

Just as there is no doubt that Jesus, the Son of God, descended from heaven to wear a crown of thorns and sacrifice his life for you, you may be certain that Jesus is alive and born in your heart *today!*

Yet to all who received him, to those who believed in his name, he gave the right to become children of God—children born not of natural descent, nor of human decision... but born of God.

—JOHN 1:12-13

ABOUT THE AUTHORS

For over twenty-five years Bodie and Brock Thoene (pronounced *Tay-nee*) have pursued advanced studies in Jewish history, concentrating on the Jewish roots of Christianity. They have been adjunct professors with The Masters College in European history, English literature, and Journalism. They also teach Writing for Publication in association with the University of the Nations, Kona, Hawaii.

Brock holds advanced degrees in History and Education. Besides being an amateur astronomer, he has made the study of biblical Hebrew his life's work. Bodie has degrees in Journalism and Communications. She began her writing career with John Wayne's Batjac Productions.

The Thoenes have written over 45 works of internationally acclaimed historical fiction—including The Zion Chronicles, The Zion Covenant, The Zion Legacy, The Shiloh Legacy, The Galway Chronicles, A.D. Chronicles, and Legends of the West—as well as regular devotional blogs and commentaries. Their weblog can be found at www.thoenebooks.com.

Their novels of pre-World War II Europe (The Zion Covenant series) and the miraculous rebirth of Israel and the Israeli War of Independence (The Zion Chronicles and The Zion Legacy series) are highly regarded for their history accuracy, recognized by the American Library Association and Zionist libraries around the world, and widely used in university classrooms to teach history.

That their books have sold more than 10 million copies and have won eight ECPA Gold Medallion awards affirms what millions of readers have already discovered—the Thoenes are not only master stylists but experts at capturing readers' minds and hearts.

Married for over 35 years, the Thoenes have four grown children and six grandchildren. Their assistance to Jews making aliyah to Israel from the countries of the former Soviet Union has been acknowledged by the nation of Israel.

Co-founded by the Thoenes, The Shiloh Light Foundation (www.shilohlightfoundation.org), ships Christian literature and Bibles to prisoners and to members of the U.S. armed forces and their families. Through www.familyaudiolibrary.com, the Foundation also produces and provides low cost Christian audiobooks to those who are visually handicapped and/or learning disabled.

For more information, visit www.thoenebooks.com.

Want to read more about the story of Jesus?

Zion Legacy, by Bodie and Brock Thoene

The Jerusalem Scrolls, The Stones of Jerusalem,
and *Jerusalem's Hope*

A mysterious prophet transforms the lives of Miryam of Magdala, Marcus the Centurion, and three Jewish orphans.

A.D. Chronicles® by Bodie and Brock Thoene

First Light
At the darkest time in Jewish history, blind beggar
Peniel longs for light...and finds the Healer.

Second Touch
Lily, the leper of the Valley of Mak'ob, discovers that
nothing is too hard for God.

Third Watch
The truth about who Jesus is transforms despair into joy
for Susanna, Manaen, Zahav, Alexander, and young Hero.

Fourth Dawn
Where is the promised liberator? Signs appear in the
heavens, and Mary receives an unusual visitor.

Fifth Seal
Is anywhere far enough from King Herod's evil clutches?

Sixth Covenant
Bethlehem becomes the focus of a terrifying rampage...
and the hinge upon which all history turns.

And more to come!

For more information, visit www.thoenebooks.com

Discover the Truth through Fiction™